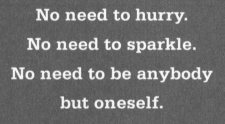

No need to hurry.
No need to sparkle.
No need to be anybody
but oneself.

—*Virginia Woolf*

Living without shame

A Support Book for Mothers with Addicted Children

52 Activities to Help You Feel, Heal, and Grow

Barbara Theodosiou

founder of The Addict's Mom community and author of *Without Shame*

and

The editors of Hazelden Publishing

Hazelden Publishing
Center City, Minnesota 55012
hazelden.org/bookstore

Library of Congress Cataloging-in-Publication Data

Theodosiou, Barbara, 1959– author.
Living without shame : a support book for mothers with addicted children : 52 activities to
    help you feel, heal, and grow / Barbara Theodosiou and the editors of Hazelden Publishing.
First Edition. | Center City : Hazelden Publishing, 2020. |
    LCCN 2019044944 | ISBN 9781616497811 (paperback)
LCSH: Parents of drug addicts—United States. | Drug addicts—United States—
    Family relationships.
LCC HV5808.T543 2020 | DDC 362.29/13—dc23
LC record available at https://lccn.loc.gov/2019044944

Editor's notes

This publication is not intended as a substitute for the advice of health care professionals. Readers should be aware that websites listed in this work may have changed or disappeared between when this work was written and when it is read.

24 23 22 21 20   1 2 3 4 5 6

Cover and interior design: Terri Kinne
Acquisitions editor: Vanessa Torrado
Editorial development: Vanessa Torrado, Heather Silsbee, and Christian Johnson
Editorial project manager: Jean Cook

Images used under license from Shutterstock.com and iStockphoto.com

This book is for

Fred, Peter, and Daniel
You've taught me the importance of a recovery of my own.
I am blessed to be part of your family.

And all women who can call themselves "the addict's mom."
Without you, my fellow moms, it would have been impossible for me to leave the path of destruction I found myself traveling.
With all of you, my sisters, I relearned the gift of the life I have been given.
Alongside all of you, I no longer take this life for granted.

Contents

You Matter: A Reminder from a Fellow Mom   2

Courage to Feel   10

Make Your Place   13

Check In with Yourself   14

Grow Gratitude   16

Mom's Time-Out   19

Take Pride   20

Sorry, Self   21

Stigma   22

Transformation   24

Be Here Now   28

At My Worst   31

At My Best   32

A Gift to Myself   34

Full of Darkness   36

Full of Light   37

Life's Expectations   39

A Heart Full of Hope   40

Look How Far I've Come   42

Honor Your Grief   45

Must Do   48

Communicate to Heal   54

A Different Type of Family Tree   56

Your Empty Well   58

Tending to Fences   61

Quitting Is Okay   64

The Wounded Healer   66

What I Like about You   68

Triggers and Reactions   71

Perfectly Imperfect Parenting   74

The First   76

The Last   78

Put a Pin in It   80

Back to the Present   82

Climb Every Mountain   84

Sleepless Nights   86

Your Value   87

Letting Go Requires More Strength Than Holding On   89

Right Now   90

Emotional Links   92

Community to Grow   98

Before and After   100

My Tribe   102

Want Ad   105

Back in Touch   106

Thank-You Card   107

It Takes a Village   108

Discover Superpowers   110

Map of Support   112

Grow with Each Other   113

Stronger Together   114

Gift of Unity   116

Self-Care Cures   117

Choose a Mentor   118

Your Shared Purpose   120

A Love Letter   123

Recommended Resources   131

Acknowledgments   137

About the Author   139

Living without shame

Recovery
is an acceptance
that your life
is in shambles
and you have to
change it.

—*Jamie Lee Curtis*

You Matter

A Reminder from a Fellow Mom

For the past several years, I've been working on two books: this book, which you have in your hands, and *Without Shame: The Addict's Mom and Her Family Share Their Stories of Pain and Healing.* The latter tells my story, my family's story; but more importantly, it tells the story of how and why my family got to where we are now. If that book shares our journey, then this book shares some of what I've learned along the way that might be helpful to other moms, to you.

It's been a difficult journey. More than a decade ago, I realized that addiction had made its way into my home. I have four children. Within a period of less than six months, I realized that two of my sons were struggling with substance abuse. One of my sons is now thriving in recovery; my other son passed away in 2015. Like all mothers, when I realized my children were suffering, the first questions I asked were "How did this happen?" and "What can I do?"

With addiction, there's no simple answer. One question brings up hundreds of other questions, many of which have very complicated responses. We want concrete "answers," just like we want concrete "fixes" to any problems our children are facing. We want a prescription for healing and wellness.

Instead of answers, we only uncover pieces of a complicated puzzle that may help guide us forward. There are no guarantees. There are just guideposts that might help us understand when and where certain things began to change shape, and more guideposts that may help us carry on.

When I started trying to understand how and why addiction had begun to take hold of my family, I started confronting things that may sound very familiar to all of you. These experiences are what led me to start The Addict's Mom (TAM) in 2008. I thought, "If I'm facing these things, there must be other mothers doing the same," and I was right. In the beginning, we were only a few dozen women trying to support each other, but we realized, even though we were very different people, we had so many experiences in common. Some of our common experiences include

- finding our children, and as a result ourselves, repeatedly in crisis

- often feeling very alone, isolated, and with nowhere to turn for help

- focusing on our addicted child so much that we neglect other people in our lives: our partners or spouses, other children, friends, parents, siblings

- having to confront a family history of addictive behaviors and how they are manifesting in the present

- accepting that addiction is a disease, not a moral failure, and letting go of our own preconceptions of addiction while battling society's preconceived notions

- learning about the disease of addiction, and its many forms of treatment, which seem to be evolving all the time

- discovering that addiction rarely exists alone; co-occurring disorders are more common than not, and getting a firm diagnosis is not always easy
- realizing that there is a stigma around this disease our children are experiencing—and that many, many people we love do not yet understand the realities that we've had to confront about addiction
- feeling like there will never be a "new normal"
- having a hard time navigating the treatment, sober living, and criminal justice systems, and sometimes feeling like they don't have the best interests of our children in mind
- being physically, emotionally, spiritually, and mentally exhausted—all at the same time—to the point of burnout
- grieving that addiction doesn't always end with a redemption story—addiction is a human story: relapses, repeated treatments, overdoses, disappearances, incarcerations, trauma, broken relationships, and more are all frequently part of our daily reality
- facing that, while we've neglected many other people in the midst of our child's addiction, we've also neglected ourselves

This final point is very important to me, which is why I listed it last. TAM has many slogans and phrases that we consistently share. The main one we repeat over and over again is that TAM is a community where we can "Share Without Shame." When people are confronted with addiction, many things that they would rather keep hidden can come to the surface. TAM is blessed with a community of tens of thousands of women who have come together to share the realities of what addiction has done to their families. The moms of TAM have realized that we are never alone with our feelings. We are all different, but we also have many things in common. In particular, we all feel the same pain. And each time one of us shares our honest truth without being judged, it makes it safer for others to do the same.

When our fight with addiction began, we all put on battle armor. We felt this armor was necessary to protect ourselves and our families from the new horrors we were facing, but then we never took it off. And that armor gets very heavy if we never take it off.

There are many life-changing lessons that I've learned from the sisterhood of TAM. But perhaps one of the most important things I've learned is that while there are times I needed to put on my armor to continue my fight against addiction, my life is more than addiction, and there are other times in my life when that armor may only weigh me down. Sharing without shame with other mothers who understand, or spending a few moments for myself when I try not to even think about addiction, can provide some much-needed rest.

The sisterhood of TAM has often had to remind me that I am more than this fight against addiction. My children's lives have been affected by the disease of addiction; my family members' lives have been affected by the disease of addiction; my life has been affected by the disease of addiction. But my life is more than this disease, and if I don't take off that battle armor from time to time, I lose touch with who I truly am and how my life has value.

Within TAM, when we share without shame with each other, we don't need that armor, because no matter how different we are, we see and feel commonalities in our experiences. We have empathy and understanding for each other and what we're going through. We reveal our unprotected vulnerability with each other, and when we do, we often recognize something in each other: We have forgotten that we matter. So, we have to remind each other of our worth, our value. We matter. We were people before we had our children; we were people before our children's lives were touched by the disease of addiction. If we give addiction all the power in our lives, we're telling ourselves that we don't matter.

Author Linda Wooten once wrote, "Being a mother is learning about strengths you didn't know you had, and dealing with fears you didn't know existed."* When we realize that our children are suffering under the weight of addiction, our worst fears become a reality. We have to deal with our fears head on, and we learn so much about ourselves as mothers, as women. But we often forget ourselves. I know I did; I still do.

It's been challenging detailing my family's journey through addiction. But I needed to do it to get back to me. By dropping my battle armor and sharing without shame, I've remembered that I matter. And I've remembered that before I can have truly healthy relationships with others, I have to have a relationship with myself. There came a time when the only relationship I was focusing on was the challenged and toxic relationship I had with addiction. I want you to remember that you matter.

* Wooten, Linda. *A Mother's Thoughts,* second edition. Amazon Digital Services, 2014.

This support book is for every mother who has found herself sitting alone in the dark, with tears running down her cheeks, feeling broken, desperate, and as if she has no one to turn to for help. I have been that mom; at my darkest moments, sisters within TAM helped me move toward the light.

These activities were designed to help you out of the darkness and back to yourself. To remember who you are and see how far you have come. To have a safe place to share. To get back on a path that nurtures and nourishes you. To recognize that you matter.

This support book was designed and written by myself and the editors at Hazelden Publishing to give mothers one activity per week that might help them realize and remember that they matter. As mothers, it can be unthinkable to take time out of our schedules just for ourselves, but I believe that everyone can take at least a few minutes each week. We not only can, we *have* to. Think of this book as your excuse to do so. This book has fifty-two activities. If you try to do one activity a week, after fifty-two weeks, or one year, our hope is that your life will be a little transformed because your relationship with yourself is in a different place.

This support book isn't about your child, or your child's addiction. It is to support you through how you experience your child's addiction. It is to support you as you embrace your own recovery.

I can hear you already: "But I'm not the addict! My child is!" I understand. I do. Maybe you don't have any substance use issues of your own. Or maybe your child's journey has helped you face your own history with substance use, mental health disorders, or compulsive patterns. Either way, your child's disease has affected you, and you feel as though you have lost pieces of yourself, don't you?

I have been there. There have been many times when I couldn't focus on anything but my addicted child. I discounted everything else in my life. I ignored myself and my other family members. When you are so involved in your addict's life, you're not honoring your own life. You behave in ways that say, "My life doesn't matter."

But you *do* matter.

Recovery is the process of regaining something that has been lost. It could be a sense of health, balance, or well-being. It could be your sense of self. I've yet to meet a mom who has sought out support in a community like TAM who hasn't described herself as exhausted, scared, or broken. Burned out. Your own recovery means healing what feels broken. Your recovery means recovering you. Your recovery means learning to live without shame again.

So, how should you use this book? We've called it a "support book" because it was developed to support you as you feel, heal, and grow. Do one activity a week, or be ambitious and do as much as you want in shorter periods of time. If one activity is particularly challenging and is making you feel stuck, go ahead and skip it and come back to it when you are in a different place. Do what feels right for you.

When I became a mom, I didn't imagine addiction would affect my family. I didn't think that I would ever lose a child. But when these things came to pass, I did know that there had to be thousands of mothers across the world just like me who didn't know where to turn. I want every mother who's an addict's mom to understand that you're important. I'm not only an addict's mom. I'm a wife, a mother, a friend, a cousin, a neighbor. I matter. And if you're an addict's mom, *you* matter. And whether your child is going through this horrible disease of addiction, whether they're getting better or they're not, it's important that you take care of yourself. Remember that you're not alone.

With love,
Barbara

Courage
to Feel

It is essential to create
a quiet space
in which to
evaluate the things in your life.

—Marie Kondo

Strength

Make Your Place

Carve out a place in your home that is just for you. It could be a corner, a whole room, or simply a chair you love. Decide to make it your perfect place to retreat to at least once a week for a few moments of alone time, reflection, and letting go. If it helps, think of it as the place you can go to focus on this support book.

What are the things you need to claim this space?

What could make the space more relaxing?

What do you need to tell your family to ensure the space is yours?

How will you enforce your boundaries and remind people it is your special place?

How will it look, feel, and smell?

How do you feel when you sit down in this space, and how do you feel when you leave?

In the space below, make notes for yourself that will get you started, and that you can refer to over time to remind you of what you wanted this space to be for you.

Check In with Yourself

When we spend so much time caregiving for others, we often lose touch with ourselves and our own feelings. Sometimes we neglect our feelings to such a degree that we start to ignore our needs, leading to exhaustion, resentment, anger, or profound sadness. One of the most important things we can do from time to time is to check in with ourselves. Rather than asking yourself how you are doing today, ask yourself what you are feeling today, so you can learn what might be behind those feelings, build your emotional vocabulary, and begin to share those feelings with others who can support you.

Check any feelings on this list that resonate with you today. Write in any other emotion words you are feeling in the blank lines provided. Then, refer back to this list whenever you need to. It's not always easy to identify our feelings.

POSITIVE FEELINGS

Balanced	Ecstatic	Considerate
Centered	Blissful	Caring
Mindful	Carefree	Kind
Humbled	Joyful	
Forgiving	Eager	Beautiful
Calm	Enthusiastic	Proud
	Energetic	Inspired
Powerful	Excited	Worthy
Strong	Inspired	Accomplished
Brave		
	Appreciative	Affectionate
Capable	Gracious	Appreciated
Confident	Grateful	Loved
	Thankful	Loving
Optimistic	Blessed	
Cheerful	Lucky	_____
Delighted		_____
Hopeful	Nourished	_____
Happy	Fulfilled	_____
Glad	Rested	_____
	Better	

14

NEGATIVE FEELINGS

- Tired
- Fatigued

- Shocked
- Astonished
- Flustered

- Envious
- Jealous
- Judgmental

- Judged
- Shamed
- Worthless
- Guilty
- Oppressed

- Ashamed
- Embarrassed
- Disgraced
- Humiliated

- Abandoned
- Isolated
- Lonely
- Alone
- Empty
- Disengaged
- Ignored

- Nervous
- Panicked
- Anxious
- Apprehensive
- Jittery
- Distressed
- Desperate

- Bothered
- Moody
- Frustrated

- Heartbroken
- Unhappy
- Sorrowful
- Depressed
- Broken
- Bereaved

- Dismayed
- Dismal
- Melancholy
- Glum
- Discouraged

- Inadequate
- Insecure
- Imperfect
- Incomplete

- Crushed
- Disillusioned
- Let down
- Hurt
- Disappointed
- Offended

- Irritable
- Annoyed
- Aggravated
- Irritated
- Impatient

- Angry
- Bitter
- Cranky
- Furious
- Grouchy

- Cautious
- Guarded

- Uncomfortable
- Awkward
- Withdrawn
- Paralyzed

- Afraid
- Scared
- Petrified
- Fearful
- Frightened

- Apologetic
- Sorry
- Regretful

- Detached
- Disconnected
- Distant
- Indifferent
- Jaded

- Ambivalent
- Unsure
- Reluctant
- Hesitant
- Uncertain

- Powerless
- Helpless
- Hopeless
- Despondent
- Bleak
- Grim

_____
_____
_____
_____

_____
_____
_____
_____

Grow Gratitude

We don't cultivate gratitude in our lives by only thinking about what we're thankful for once a year. Gratitude can become a daily practice, starting today. By focusing on what we're grateful for at least one moment every day—rather than what we've lost, or are scared of losing—we slowly start to recognize all the positive things in our lives.

On these pages, write down something you are grateful for right now. Then, keep returning here when you pick up your support book. Try to make it a regular practice to express your gratitude.

Knowing how to be solitary
is central to the art of loving.
When we can be alone,
we can be with others
without using them
as a means of escape.

—Bell Hooks

Self-care
isn't
selfish

Mom's Time-Out

When was the last time you spent a significant amount of time alone, just enjoying your own company or doing something you care about (other than caring for others!)? When we put the needs of others ahead of our own, it's common to slowly cut back on hobbies, passions, activities, and even uninterrupted alone time. You've set up a place in your home that's just for you.

Now, put yourself in an official time-out once in a while to get to know yourself again. What are the things you miss doing just for yourself? What interests have you given up over time, not because you outgrew them, but because you focused your time on a loved one's addiction?

List ten things that you miss doing by yourself, or small things you have always wanted to try doing, that would spark joy in your life.

1 _____

2 _____

3 _____

4 _____

5 _____

6 _____

7 _____

8 _____

9 _____

10 _____

Take Pride

When my kids were little, it wasn't always easy for us. At one point I was a single mom with three children. It often felt like we were doing nothing but surviving. When we would spend time together at the beginning or end of each day, I often used to ask my kids to tell me things that they had done that day that made them proud. It helped us feel more like we were thriving rather than just surviving.

At the peak of my sons' addictions, when I felt myself becoming little more than "the addict's mom," I found myself in survival mode again. I ceased being me. I stopped living.

By taking pride in ourselves, our actions, and our day-to-day life, we pay attention to ourselves again. We re-emerge as people. We start thriving again.

What are five things you've done or said recently that make you feel proud of yourself?

1

2

3

4

5

Sorry, Self

Shame is often accompanied by feelings of low self-worth. That is, sometimes we let the shame other people cast on us take our power because we're already not feeling very powerful, valuable, or worthy. Learning to be gentle with ourselves is a big step forward in feeling a sense of inner peace. Sometimes it feels like we're always apologizing to other people for things we've done or for who we are. When it comes to addiction's impact on our family, we often apologize to those around us for how our loved one's addiction has impacted them. But when was the last time you apologized to yourself?

List five times when you were too hard on yourself, expected too much of yourself, thought too little of yourself, allowed someone to push you too far, or generally mistreated yourself. Then say, "Sorry, self!"

1 _____

_____

2 _____

_____

3 _____

_____

4 _____

_____

5 _____

_____

The biggest paradox:
To be happy, surrender to what hurts.
Forgiveness isn't a one-time deal.
The need to make peace is ongoing.

—Melody Beattie

Stigma

There's such stigma around the diseases and disorders that impact millions of families: addiction, substance use disorders, mental health conditions, and co-occurring disorders. But "stigma" is just another word for "shame." Often we're so busy just trying to survive that we try to ignore the shame that we feel. Ignoring our shame often increases it, which can lead to a growing sense of resentment with the people who made us feel the shame. Take the time to start sifting through feelings of shame you are carrying.

Can you think of three instances in which you feel or have felt shame in response to people's reactions or aspects of the diseases affecting your family?

1 _____

_____

_____

_____

2 _____

_____

_____

_____

3 _____

_____

_____

_____

**You may not control
all the events that happen to you,
but you can decide
not to be reduced by them.**

—Maya Angelou

Transformation

The Addict's Mom was founded to be a place to "Share Without Shame." If having someone hear you and empathize with you will transform your shame into courage and strength, then share your story with someone you trust. You've written down three instances in which you and your family feel shame about addiction and other diseases. Acknowledging the feelings of shame is the first step. Writing down the stories surrounding those feelings can help us better understand them ourselves.

Use the following three pages to draft the stories around the three situations in which you feel shame about addiction and other disorders. When you feel ready, share one of these stories with someone you trust.

I felt shame about addiction and other disorders when . . .

I felt shame about addiction and other disorders when . . .

I felt shame about addiction and other disorders when . . .

My story . . .

If we can share our story
with someone who responds
with empathy and
understanding,
shame can't survive.

—Brené Brown

Empathy

Be Here Now

Mindfulness can be defined as a state of conscious awareness of the present. It's common to get lost in our own thoughts and feelings. Too often we focus our energy on what could have been or what will be. Or we focus on what others around us are doing or what we think they need. Sometimes it's easier to focus on the past or our dreams for the future than to face what we are feeling right now. But being focused on the past or the future prevents us from truly living. The only time we can control is right now. By focusing only on the present moment, we can learn to pay attention to our surroundings, our feelings, and our needs. We can finally take steps to let go of things that we cannot control.

Close your eyes. Take several deep breaths. Imagine that any tension you have in your neck, your jaw, your back, your hands, your legs, and your feet is leaving your body. Now open your eyes. Look around the room.

What do you see? Are there details you have never noticed before? What color is most prominent in the room? Does the way the room looks make you feel calm or anxious? What would you change to make it more calming?

What do you hear? Is there a repeating sound that grabs your attention?
Are there sounds you hear through the window closest to you?
How do you feel when you hear those sounds?

What do you smell? Is there something around you that produces a
pleasant scent? Is it something you chose for your space, like a candle or
essential oils? Or was it something someone perhaps gave you, such as
flowers? Do the smells create happy memories for you, or do they lead
to challenging feelings?

Use this exercise to bring yourself back to the present whenever you feel
overwhelmed by stress or anxiety.

That's life: starting over, one breath at a time.

—Sharon Salzberg

The most common way
people give up their power
is by thinking
they don't have any.

—Alice Walker

One day
at a
time

At My Worst

Right now, you may not feel like your best self. In fact, you might not even feel like yourself at all. Take a moment to dig deep and capture what you've felt like at your worst. Maybe it was when you felt weakest, or at your lowest point. Or perhaps it was when you were caregiving for everyone around you, but had not even taken a moment to feed, bathe, or care for yourself. Did you catch a glimpse of yourself in a mirror or a photograph and not recognize yourself? Capture the details below to remind yourself how and why things got that far.

At My Best

You've remembered what it felt like to be at your worst. Now, even if you don't feel like your best self in this moment, think back to a time when you *did* feel at your best. Maybe you felt accomplished or strong. Did you face a fear and suddenly feel confident? Capture the details below to get in touch with that part of yourself again.

_____

_____

_____

_____

_____

_____

_____

_____

_____

_____

Remember, all of these amazing things are part of who you are and they always will be. Nothing can ever take them away from you.

The dark does not destroy the light;
it defines it.
It's our fear of the dark
that casts our joy
into the shadows.

—Brené Brown

Confidence

A Gift to Myself

Shortly after I found out that two of my sons were suffering from the disease of addiction, I attended a local support group meeting. During the meeting, I sat quietly and listened, but never contributed. The tears that streamed down my face the entire meeting probably spoke volumes. At the end of the meeting, another mom approached me, put her hand on my shoulder, and pronounced—it kind of felt like an order—the following: "Remember your self-care."

I have to admit that at the time, I had a complicated relationship with self-care. I didn't truly know what "self-care" was. But shortly after that meeting, I caught sight of myself in a hallway mirror. At first I didn't recognize myself. There were dark circles under my eyes that no makeup could begin to cover because I was rarely sleeping through the night, always waiting for the next call bringing another emergency. I'd got into the habit of wearing the same sweatpants and T-shirt for resting and running errands, so I had been wearing the same clothes for days. I wasn't showering, styling my hair, or even eating nourishing foods.

It became difficult to ignore the reflection of what I'd become, which helped me understand what my fellow mom meant at that support meeting. I wasn't tending to myself—I was focused solely on my sons and their addictions. Addiction's grip on *my sons* had also taken over *my life*. I had forgotten my self-care. I had forgotten myself entirely.

Our survival matters. Our lives matter. Realizing that I mattered was how I understood "self-care."

Self-care is how you take your power back.

—Lalah Delia

You matter. What are ten ways you will care for yourself on a regular basis going forward?

1 _____

_____

2 _____

_____

3 _____

_____

4 _____

_____

5 _____

_____

6 _____

_____

7 _____

_____

8 _____

_____

9 _____

_____

10 _____

_____

Full of Darkness

What are ten things that fill you with feelings of
sadness, despair, or sorrow?

1

2

3

4

5

6

7

8

9

10

Full of Light

What are ten things that fill you with feelings of
joy, happiness, and well-being?

1 _____

2 _____

3 _____

4 _____

5 _____

6 _____

7 _____

8 _____

9 _____

10 _____

Letting go of expectations is fundamental to recovery for most families.

Only then can we stop projecting and worrying about the outcome of things.

—Beverly Conyers

Growth

Life's Expectations

Many times, our fears come from expectations we have for situations, people, and our lives. There's a difference between hopes and expectations. We can hope something will happen without demanding that it occur however and whenever we want it to. Expectations are rigid and inflexible outcomes we carry within ourselves—sometimes consciously and sometimes unconsciously. When we identify the expectations we carry in life, we can prepare to let them go and replace them with healthier hopes.

What expectations do you have for yourself, your life, and your family that you think you should let go?

A Heart Full of Hope

While expectations are rigid, hope is flexible. Hope is influenced by our dreams, imagination, and feelings of love. Our hopes are responsive to what is happening in our lives and keep us focused on the positive things that could happen. Hope leads us to see changes in life as opportunities for growth and transformation, and it leaves us feeling energized. When we identify the hopes in our hearts, we feel full of life and potential.

What hopes do you carry for yourself, your life, and your family?

I taught myself to believe
that no matter what
I felt or what happened
when I felt it,
I would be okay.

—Iyanla Vanzant

Potential

Look How Far I've Come

Across a lifetime, we face many obstacles, challenges, fears, and worries. Sometimes, realizing how we faced challenges in the past helps us move forward.

What challenges did you face

. . . twenty years ago?

_____

_____

. . . fifteen years ago?

_____

_____

. . . ten years ago?

_____

_____

. . . five years ago?

_____

_____

. . . this year?

_____

_____

And what steps did you take to overcome these obstacles

. . . twenty years ago?

_____

_____

. . . fifteen years ago?

_____

_____

. . . ten years ago?

_____

_____

. . . five years ago?

_____

_____

. . . this year?

_____

_____

> **We learned, or began to learn,**
> **how to detach with love.**
> **It was a new language**
> **that we could speak to each other**
> **—a safe and powerful language.**
>
> —Alex and Pedro Alba

When a problem first appears,
we think we're the only one who has it.

We feel alone.

Before long, it looks like there's
an epidemic going on.

We wait for life to be like it was,
then one day we get it:

Life as we know it is gone. It's never
going to be the same again . . .

Grief is a sacred time in our lives,
and an important one.

— Melody Beattie

Change

Honor Your Grief

In her book *The Grief Club,* Melody Beattie details how we experience grief over so many different types of loss and change. We grieve when a loved one passes away. When a loved one is diagnosed with a chronic illness or disease. When we're diagnosed with a health condition or illness. When expectations we held dear do not come to fruition. When trauma we've experienced impacts us years later. When relationships come to an end. When loved ones go missing or experience trauma. When we experience financial hardship. When loved ones are incarcerated . . . the list goes on. Sometimes we realize we are still holding on to losses that seem small in comparison to things we have experienced since. Unpacking the many things we grieve helps us identify and honor our feelings.

What do you grieve, big and small?

What do you grieve, big and small?

What do you grieve, big and small?

Must Do

Addiction and co-occurring disorders in our family often lead us to put everything on the back burner, taking a lot of joy out of our lives. Sometimes we never return to things we feel are important, which leaves us feeling regret.

What hopes, dreams, or experiences are so important to you that you want to make them come true, no matter what?

When you recover
or discover something
that nourishes your soul
and brings joy, care
enough about yourself
to make room for it
in your life.

—Jean Shinoda Bolen

Nourish
yourself

My Thoughts . . .

My Thoughts . . .

My Thoughts . . .

My Thoughts . . .

Communicate
to Heal

A Different Type of Family Tree

I was always very up-front with my children about addiction, substance use, and mental health. I never hid the realities of addiction or depression from them. It was a decision I made when they were young, because I witnessed both within my family. When we were first contacted by my son's school—they suspected he was using drugs—the questions began shortly after. Is there a family history? It's uncomfortable and painful at times to build our family trees from the perspective of the diseases to which we're prone or susceptible. But information is power. Early intervention and good, proactive care are important parts of wellness.

Think of your family tree. Are there family members you know, or you suspect, had substance use issues or mental health disorders? On a leaf, write your family member's name and, if you wish, the person's relationship to you, and the diagnosed or suspected issue.

Your Empty Well

Many of us experience burnout and exhaustion as moms of people contending with addiction, alcoholism, or co-occurring disorders. In a society where we're told "moms can do it all," we often take on too much, only to find ourselves running on an empty tank.

What are ten things, experiences, interactions, or practices that would help you fill your depleted well?

1

2

3

4

5

I do not fix problems. I fix my thinking.
Then problems fix themselves.

—Louise Hay

6 _____

_____

_____

7 _____

_____

_____

8 _____

_____

_____

9 _____

_____

_____

10 _____

_____

_____

How could sharing these needs with others help you?

_____

_____

_____

_____

_____

Love yourself enough
to set boundaries.
Your time and energy
are precious.
You get to choose
how you use it.
You teach people how to
treat you by deciding what
you will and won't accept.

— Anna Taylor

Tending to Fences

Establishing boundaries is one of the most important lessons that addiction and co-occurring disorders can teach us. In her seminal book *Boundaries: Where You End and I Begin,* Anne Katherine writes, "Our emotional health is related to the health of our boundaries . . . Where are your boundaries? Do you know? Do you have a sense of your edges, your uniqueness? Are you comfortable with your limits?" *

It takes getting to know ourselves and developing our self-awareness to understand our boundaries, but it takes practice, patience, and a true desire to grow our relationships to communicate our boundaries to others.

When a loved one's addiction or mental health is in crisis, we often find ourselves in situations we'd never imagined. We also sometimes find ourselves doing things that aren't "normal" for us. Sometimes we say, "Just this once" or "I have to do this to make sure they are okay." But we are often left feeling like we have crossed the lines of what is acceptable to ourselves, or that our loved ones have crossed the line with us.

Tending to our fences means tending to the limits of our emotional health and well-being. On the following pages, try to capture instances in which either you or someone you care for crossed your boundaries. What will you do differently next time? How can you communicate your boundaries to that person, or enforce your boundaries for yourself?

* Katherine, Anne. *Boundaries: Where You End and I Begin.*
  Center City, Minnesota: Hazelden Publishing, 1991.

Name a hole in your fence that you need to tend to. Name an instance when someone crossed a boundary recently. How have you crossed your own boundaries? How can you communicate your boundaries?

Name a hole in your fence that you need to tend to. Name an instance when someone crossed a boundary recently. How have you crossed your own boundaries? How can you communicate your boundaries?

Quitting Is Okay

It's really only when the levee breaks that we begin to realize we're over-scheduled, overcommitted, and trying to be everything to everyone. When we experience a significant change in life—or many in a row—such as contending with the fact that addiction has affected our family, one of the reasons we begin to feel burnout is that we're neglecting to adjust to the new normal. Sometimes our circumstances would be calmer and more manageable if we scaled back on our commitments. That's right: Sometimes we need to quit things to which we've previously committed.

What are your current commitments? Are there a handful of items you could take a raincheck on, postpone, or hand over to other people? Try to identify at least three things that would simplify your weekly schedule.

1

2

3

How can you communicate your streamlined plan to those involved?

_____

_____

_____

_____

_____

_____

_____

_____

_____

_____

**Even if the addict is not ready to embrace recovery,
families can begin their own journey at any time.
In fact, when the family begins to get well,
interpersonal dynamics change,
often sparking the desire for recovery in the addict.**

—Beverly Conyers

The Wounded Healer

As mothers, we spend a lot of time helping our loved ones heal. When a child gets sick, we often drop everything to make them better. Because many of us aren't doctors, we discount our role in the healing process. But it's important to acknowledge that so many of us assume the role of "family healer." We make appointments, we research treatments, we administer medication, we know just from our loved one's face or breathing if he or she is healing or worsening. We understand and watch every sign. That means we assume a partial role as a healer.

When addiction makes its way into our family, we try responding the same way. Once again, we drop everything and try to heal the person suffering with this disease. While addiction is a family disease, it is also a disease that can only truly be managed by the person afflicted with it.

As the person who often assumes the role of "family caregiver" or healer, it's a challenging conundrum. Your recipe for chicken soup or your famous grilled cheese that your kids asked you for whenever they were ill is not going to heal things in the addiction landscape. But we follow our motherly instincts. Even if we end up a wounded healer.

Healing ourselves requires us to understand our own behaviors and patterns—and change them if need be. Can you think of times you continued trying to heal your child's co-occurring disorders or addiction, even when you knew it wasn't yours to heal? What were the results?

The therapy team had to train me,
the parent, that my son had the abilities
to figure things out on his own.

On a pink piece of paper,
I wrote down phrases
such as "I'm sure
you can figure it out"
and "I have confidence
in you."

—Sarah McDade

Letting go

What I Like about You

We all need and like to receive affirmation from others, but one of the most important things we can do is *give ourselves* affirmation and kindness. The messages we communicate to ourselves, consciously and unconsciously, are perhaps more important than the ones we hear from others.

Imagine yourself standing in front of a mirror. Really look at yourself, inside and out. What are ten things you really like about yourself and who you are?

1

2

3

4

5

6 _____

_____

_____

7 _____

_____

_____

8 _____

_____

_____

9 _____

_____

_____

10 _____

_____

_____

Embrace and love all of yourself—past, present, and future.
Forgive yourself quickly and as often as necessary.
Encourage yourself.
Tell yourself good things about yourself.

—Melody Beattie

What would it be
like if I could
accept life—accept
this moment—
exactly as it is?

—Tara Brach

Acceptance

Triggers and Reactions

Think about reactions you have had to situations you've experienced with your loved ones, friends, or colleagues. Have there been times when your responses have surprised you, or you've had reactions that you regret? When life becomes challenging, it's common to react in ways that are more pronounced than usual. Such reactions are usually because our emotions have been "triggered." Sometimes our reactions are our first sign that we are sensitive to an issue, and exploring them—and discussing our reactions with others—is an important step forward with ourselves and our relationships. Common triggers can include feeling disrespected, taken advantage of, abandoned, ignored, or unheard—among others. For parents of children suffering with addiction or co-occurring disorders, watching the nuclear family and its traditions fall apart can be very triggering.

When we take the time to analyze our reactions, we're better able to catch and prevent unhealthy responses, and we put ourselves in a position of strength for communicating our needs to others.

Can you think of times when your emotions have felt triggered? Who was there? What did you feel? How did you react? Would you handle the situation differently now? How could you explain the reasons for your reaction to the person you were interacting with to try to move things forward in a positive way in the future? Use the following pages to explore these questions.

Triggers and Reactions

SITUATION 1

What happened

My reaction

Who was involved

How I felt

What I could do differently

What I want those involved to know

Triggers and Reactions

SITUATION 2

What happened

My reaction

Who was involved

How I felt

What I could do differently

What I want those involved to know

Perfectly Imperfect Parenting

There's no such thing as a perfect parent. Despite all the advice we may have heard from others, there is no one "right" way to parent. Parenting isn't "one size fits all"—we all do things differently. The thing we all have in common is that we love our children unconditionally and do our best to make sure they know that. When substance use or co-occurring disorders affect our family, however, we begin to think that *if we had done something differently or had been a better parent,* our loved ones would have been immune to such a disease. In other words, even though we rationally know there is no such thing as a *perfect* parent, we begin to judge ourselves and assume that "If I were perfect, this would not have happened."

Think of three examples that might be best described as "perfectly imperfect parenting" that are part of your history as a parent. Detail them here.

"Perfectly imperfect parenting" example 1:

_____

_____

_____

"Perfectly imperfect parenting" example 2:

_____

_____

_____

"Perfectly imperfect parenting" example 3:

_____

_____

_____

Now share your three examples with a trusted friend. Do you think any parents are "perfect," or are all parents imperfect people trying to do the best possible job as people, mothers, and fathers?

_____

_____

_____

_____

_____

_____

_____

_____

_____

_____

_____

_____

**Imperfect parenting does not cause children
to become addicts. If that were so,
every child in the world would grow up to be one.**

—Sandra Swenson

The First

What's your first memory of alcohol or drug use? How did you feel when using, and who was involved?

If there's one thing I learned in Al-Anon, it's that you got to face the music because it just grows louder when you ignore it.

—Vicki Covington

Memories

The Last

What's your most recent memory of alcohol or drug use? How did you feel when using, and who was involved?

It wasn't
so much about
breaking free
of him,
as it was
about breaking
free of me.

—Grace W. Wroldson

New
beginnings

Put a Pin in It

We talk a lot about having to learn to let go. But there's also a time to hold on to special feelings, things, and memories. The expression "put a pin in it" sounds deflating—as if we're going to burst a bubble to make it disappear. But what it actually means is that we're going to pin something to keep it for later. When addiction comes into our family, we often feel like it has stolen important parts of our family from us. When things are stolen, we often feel unable to share these important pieces of ourselves with others.

What memories, feelings, or events do you feel it's important to "put a pin in" to keep them safe for later? Write some of them in the boxes below. If you're feeling creative, you could also draw, glue, or tape reminders of special memories.

Back to the Present

Technology can be a lifesaver. But it can also be a distraction from the present. When we worry about a loved one's addiction and health, it can often feel like our cell phone or devices are our only way of knowing—and checking—if everything is okay. But technology can also get in the way of living and communicating. How many times a day do you pick up your phone or device? Do you answer a call from your loved one even when you are in the middle of an important task or when it's an inconvenient time? Are your devices getting in the way of your other relationships or communication in general? Do you feel the need to check on things or take calls even when you know you shouldn't be?

Put a check mark by all of the occasions when you have checked your device recently:

- as soon as I wake up
- while I'm commuting
- while I'm waiting in lines
- at red lights and stop signs
- before I fall asleep
- in the middle of the night
- at dinner with loved ones
- while doing laundry
- while spending time with friends
- at the movies
- on the phone with others

- in the middle of recitals or events
- while I'm at work
- when I'm exercising
- at meals
- when checking out at the store
- at events for my other children
- at the doctor's office
- as a passenger in a car with others

This week, try to be mindful of this behavior and resist the urge to check when you should be focused on something or someone else.

When we are not emotionally present,
we are gliding over the surface
of our interactions and we never tangle
in the depths where the nuances
of our skills are tested and refined.

—Marian Deegan

Be present

Climb Every Mountain

The challenges you have faced with your child's addiction have likely been some of the most serious of your life; however, your child's addiction is not your addiction. Describe the story of the "steepest" mountain you've climbed, the biggest challenge you have surmounted. How do you think your experience could help others?

Tell the story of the mountain you climbed.
Your words could become a page
in someone else's survival guide.

—Morgan Harper Nichols

Overcome

Sleepless Nights

Feeling rested is a core component to real wellness and balance. When we're not sleeping, our stress levels soar, our reactions are heightened, our communication with others breaks down—and this all becomes a vicious cycle.

What are some of the things you've been doing to try to sleep through the night? Are there extremes you are going to in order to get some rest that you need to tell your family or a medical professional about? How can your family and loved ones support you in regularly getting a good night's sleep?

**Sometimes the most important thing in a whole day
is the rest we take between two deep breaths.**

—Etty Hillesum

Your Value

One day, after I had my children, my father approached me and said, "You finally understand your value." He didn't mean that motherhood and being a wife gave me a purpose; he meant that in the chaos of caring for my children, my husband, and my family, I had begun to push back on what wasn't right for me. I spoke up more when I thought people didn't treat me in a way I deserved; I enforced my boundaries. These things disappeared when addiction infiltrated my home. I let addiction take away my consent. There came a time when I had to remind myself that I matter, that I have value. So, I sat down and made a list—something moms often do for errands.

Here's your errand: List three things that remind you of your value as a person.

1 _____

_____

_____

2 _____

_____

_____

3 _____

_____

_____

**No one can make you feel inferior
without your consent.**

—Eleanor Roosevelt

In letting go of you,
I'm letting you know
that I believe in you.

—Sandra Swenson

Detach with love

Letting Go Requires More Strength
Than Holding On

We've always been told that the strong keep trying. We should get up and try again. But with addiction, we're told we need to learn to let go. It's one of the hardest lessons to learn.

Fill the balloons on this page with the things you keep putting energy toward that aren't really yours to fix, manage, heal, or tend to. Are there things you are doing, and just not giving up on, that do not seem to be working out? Is it time to let go?

Right Now

If you wanted people to remember one thing about you right now, in the present moment, what would it be?

_____

_____

_____

_____

_____

_____

How many people know this about you? What are some ways you can try to show this defining part of yourself more often?

_____

_____

_____

_____

_____

_____

Our collective stories and experiences can be the greatest textbooks of life. But with every shameful story stuffed away, we bypass the chance to expand and connect—a missed opportunity slipped through our fingers.

—Kristen Noel

Connect

Emotional Links

Resentments build up over time. Sometimes we can, with laser precision, identify pain and trauma that we've been carrying around. Other times, years of "paper cuts" we've sustained build up and fill us with bitterness. Either way, these resentments control us. When a child is contending with the disease of addiction, our hurts, traumas, and resentments seem to multiply faster than we realize. Each resentment is a heavy link in a chain that weighs us down. Our work is to identify these resentments—whether or not they are related to our child's addiction or co-occurring disorder—and begin to set ourselves free.

List ten resentments for which you have been making space in your life. As you name the pain you've incurred, also forgive the person or situation that prompted your emotional reaction.

1

2

3

4

5

6

7

8

9

10

**When you hold resentment toward another,
you are bound to that person or condition
by an emotional link that is stronger than steel.**

**Forgiveness is the only way to dissolve
that link and get free.**

—Catherine Ponder

My Thoughts . . .

My Thoughts . . .

My Thoughts . . .

My Thoughts . . .

Community
to Grow

Before and After

Think of your life ten years ago. Were there people you talked with every day, people you spent your free time with, or members of your family you considered part of your "family of friends"? There are so many strong representations of women and their "squads" now. Thinking back, before addiction affected your family, who was part of your "squad"? Starting from the central circle below that's labeled "Me," use the circles that grow from the middle of the page to identify the people who were the closest to you and the farthest from you within your social and family circle ten years ago.

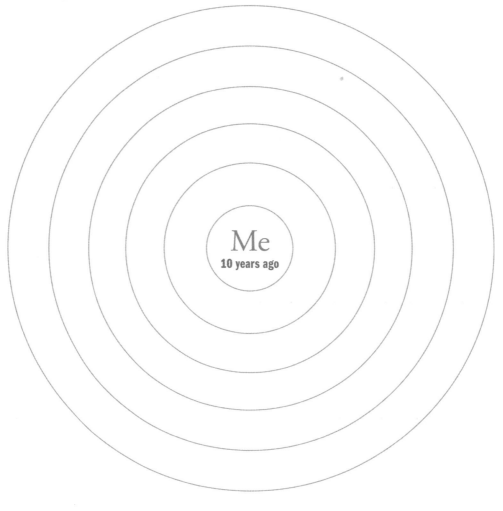

Think of your life now. Who is in your "squad"? Which squad members are you closest to? Which ones do you talk to every day or take your problems to? Are there friends and family members with whom you spend the most time? Starting from the central circle below that's labeled "Me," use the circles that grow from the middle of the page to identify the people who are closest to you and farthest from you within your social and family circle today.

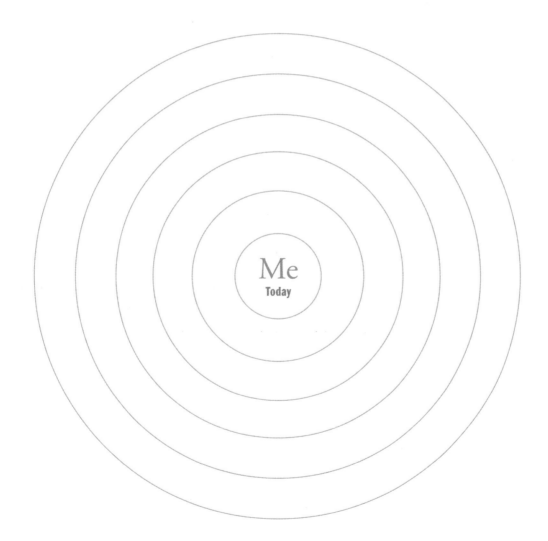

Me
Today

My Tribe

We all have people who make us feel comfortable. When our family is affected by addiction, one of the things that can happen is that we find ourselves turning away from those who used to provide us with the most comfort and friendship. Members of our "squad" may no longer relate to what we're going through, or we may not want to bring the shadows of addiction to those relationships. At that time, we often feel the need to grow our "tribe"—find people with similar experiences who don't need us to explain our current situation. While our "squad" might know us best, members of our "tribe" might relate easier to our experiences with our children. Some members of your new tribe might be blood relatives, others are chosen family, and some might be colleagues or members of a support community. Who is part of your tribe?

Name: _____

How do you connect with this person? Do you talk to them in person, on the phone, or through a support group?

_____

_____

What are some things you talk about with this member of your tribe that you don't feel comfortable bringing to members of your old squad?

_____

_____

Never doubt that a small group of thoughtful, committed citizens can change the world; indeed, it's the only thing that ever has.

—Margaret Mead

Name: _____

How do you connect with this person? Do you talk to them in person, on the phone, or through a support group?

_____

_____

What are some things you talk about with this member of your tribe that you don't feel comfortable bringing to members of your old squad?

_____

_____

_____

Name: _____

How do you connect with this person? Do you talk to them in person, on the phone, or through a support group?

_____

_____

What are some things you talk about with this member of your tribe that you don't feel comfortable bringing to members of your old squad?

_____

_____

_____

**Find a group of people who
challenge and inspire you;
spend a lot of time with them,
and it will change your life.**

—Amy Poehler

Want Ad

Major life changes can lead to entirely new life experiences for which we're unprepared. When I realized my sons were struggling with addiction, I didn't have anyone to talk to about what I was experiencing, what my sons were experiencing, what my family was experiencing. So, I formed a new support group—The Addict's Mom—to find people who were experiencing similar things.

If you had to place an advertisement for the type of support system, network, or people who might be able to support you, empathize with what you are going through, and even bring some fun into your life, how would you want the ad to read?

Back in Touch

Along the way, we often lose touch with people who have mattered to us or supported us. After having looked at how your closest community has evolved in the past decade, find one person with whom you've lost touch. Write them a draft of a letter. Tell them why you miss them and how much you valued their friendship.

Will you take the time to turn your draft into a letter, and send it?

Thank-You Card

Think of five things people have done for you recently for which you are grateful. List them here, noting what they did or why you appreciate it, and then write those people a letter of thanks.

1 _____
  _____
  _____

2 _____
  _____
  _____

3 _____
  _____
  _____

4 _____
  _____
  _____

5 _____
  _____
  _____

I would rather walk with a friend in the dark, than alone in the light.

—Helen Keller

It Takes a Village

Moms are full of superpowers. We know that. Over time, as a parent, even if no one pats us on the back for it, we find ourselves handling situations we never thought possible. There's grace in the chaos. But at times the chaos overtakes the grace. We find ourselves up against situations that we simply cannot handle alone. When we realize we might not even know where to start in tackling a problem, we have to fall back on the old saying that sometimes it takes a village. Admitting we can't do everything, or that we don't know everything, is simply part of life. Part of our growth. And part of finding a sense of balance and well-being.

Think of ten times in the past decade when you found guidance, support, love, and mentorship by taking your challenges to a village of people.

1 _____

_____

_____

2 _____

_____

_____

3 _____

_____

_____

4 _____

_____

_____

5 _____

_____

_____

6 _____

_____

_____

7 _____

_____

_____

8 _____

_____

_____

9 _____

_____

_____

10 _____

_____

_____

**There is no power for change greater than a community
discovering what it cares about.**

—Margaret J. Wheatley

Discover Superpowers

Focusing on the strengths and talents of others can help us discover parts of ourselves we want to build and grow. It can also help us learn what parts of ourselves we might not be interested in developing. But most importantly, it can help us strengthen our bonds with our community.

Pick an acquaintance, friend, or member of your community who has always intrigued you, and ask if you can spend some time getting to know her better. Use the space below to plan out questions you want to ask her. Plan on exploring with her insights she might have on self-care, the importance of boundaries, and how she overcame her biggest obstacles. You might just discover that a member of your tribe has experienced many things from which you can learn.

The Addict's Mom
came together because
we were a group
of women with
a common
problem.

We could talk
with each other
and get to the
heart of things in
a way that wouldn't
be possible among
a general group of
women.

We could empower
each other because we
had things in common.
With other people in
your corner, all trying
to fight the same
disease, you have a
bond. You become
stronger.

—Barbara Theodosiou

Empowerment

Map of Support

Is your community close-knit geographically, or are you spread out across many states or even the country? Some of our best friends live next door; some may live across the country. It's now so easy to keep in touch with long-distance friends that we may forget we also need people close by to lean on in an emergency. Use the space below to map where your support system is located.

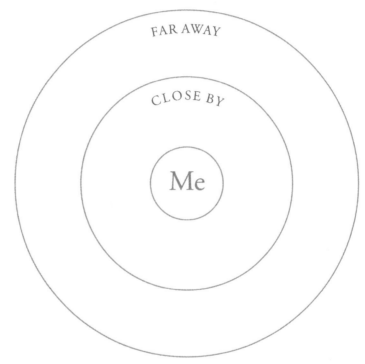

Put a star next to the two people you most want to talk to when you're in crisis. Are either of these people close by? If not, think about the people in your local area. Which of these people would you most trust if you needed to see someone right now? Circle that person. If you don't have someone you trust close by, think about how you can nurture a closer connection.

Distance cannot matter—ours is a friendship of the heart.

—Mary Anne Radmacher

Grow with Each Other

A tribe, a community, supports itself and supports its members; it doesn't seek to make each other feel small, inadequate, full of shame, or wrong. In this age, we belong to a lot of different communities, and sometimes we don't even realize how many.

Think about the online social networks that you are a part of or where you frequently spend time. How do you feel after you've been on social media? Are you really part of a community online, or do members of your community make you feel less than supported?

Our tribes, our communities, our squads, and our networks need to be built carefully, mindfully, and thoughtfully over time. And like our boundary fences, they need to be tended to from time to time.

Spend some time on your social media networks. Are there groups or individuals you feel tear you down more than they build you up? Are they the best use of your time and energy?

List five online contacts or groups to which you once felt connected but that no longer spark growth and a sense of community for you.

Name: _____

Organization: _____

Name: _____

Organization: _____

Name: _____

Organization: _____

Name: _____

Organization: _____

Name: _____

Organization: _____

Stronger Together

We all have our individual strengths and talents. When we unite those gifts with the strengths of others, we find ourselves stronger than before. Some challenges are best faced as part of a group.

Think of some examples from your history when you were stronger and more impactful as part of a group.

By reaching out to help someone who feels
every bit as helpless as we do;
by reaching out to help someone going
through a rough patch;
by saying or doing something,
anything, that might help someone
to head off on a better course—
we, each one of us,
have the power to send love and hope
outward in ripples and waves.

—Sandra Swenson

Gift of Unity

As you've grown closer and more inspired by members of your community, you may have found or thought of some symbols that represent the bonds you've established. Whether they are tokens of appreciation, items that capture moments you have shared together, or handmade crafts that express what you've shared with your tribe, it's time to show your closest tribe how much you care.

Pick at least three people you've relied on in the past year as you've found a recovery of your own who have all shared in a special moment of your healing process. Think of a small gift to give them that will capture the spirit of how they supported you and how much it means to you. Brainstorm your ideas below.

Name: _____

Healing moment: _____
_____

Possible gift: _____

Name: _____

Healing moment: _____
_____

Possible gift: _____

Name: _____

Healing moment: _____
_____

Possible gift: _____

Self-Care Cures

Finding your own recovery includes acknowledging your own need for self-care. As you've focused on your development, boundaries, and needs in the recent past, it's time to pay it forward and spread the love. Share with your community your tips for a self-care practice.

Tip:

Tip:

Tip:

Tip:

Tip:

Choose a Mentor

You've grown your community and explored the strengths members of your tribe have called upon to overcome life's biggest challenges. As you continue to grow, heal, and feel, some of your greatest breakthrough moments might come from calling upon a mentor you admire and respect.

Mentors are important in all walks of life. We need them in school and in our careers. Why wouldn't we look for one when we're still trying to manage life's most complicated moments—such as addiction?

Addiction is a family disease, which means it is also a community disease; it's also a disease that has existed as long as people have lived. We have a lot to learn from each other's recovery process, how other parents have managed their child's disease, and how people have contended with their illness.

Think about people you admire within your community. List their names, and reasons you think they would be a good mentor, in the space below.

Name: _____

would be a good mentor because

_____

_____

_____

_____

_____

_____

Name: _____

would be a good mentor because

_____

_____

_____

_____

_____

_____

Name: _____

would be a good mentor because

_____

_____

_____

_____

_____

When you feel ready, reach out to them and ask them if they could honor you with some of their time—and wisdom.

**A mentor is someone who allows you
to see the hope inside yourself.**

—Oprah Winfrey

Your Shared Purpose

When Francis Scott Key sat down to write the poem that became our national anthem, "The Star-Spangled Banner," the goal was to give his community a shared memory and vision of what they'd fought for and endured. His words were meant to inspire hope, unity, pride, and purpose. Anthems are a powerful call to collective action because they remind us of what we accomplish together.

As you've developed a community and network of parents who have also been affected by a family member's addiction, you've shared similar situations, concerns, and challenges. How would you describe your community's shared purpose? If you had to write an anthem for families that have been affected by addiction and co-occurring disorders, what would it include? If you would like to try, consider writing your anthem in the form of poetry or song lyrics.

What song or type of music would you use for your anthem?

The best thing to do
with the best things in life
is to give them away.

—Dorothy Day

Purpose

Sometimes a person just needs
a little inspiration or a different thought
to get them propelled in the right direction.

—Tondeleya Allen

A Love Letter

Knowing that you are not alone and that you are part of a community, a tribe that is stronger together, write a letter—a type of love letter—to those who support you and have your unwavering support.

Will you share your letter with your group, especially when they might need it most?

My Thoughts . . .

My Thoughts . . .

My Thoughts . . .

My Thoughts . . .

My Thoughts . . .

Hope is a renewable option:
if you run out of it at the end of the day,
you get to start over in the morning.

—Barbara Kingsolver

Hope

Recommended Resources

INFORMATIONAL

Addiction barrages us with questions: How do I get my child into treatment? How can I support their recovery? How can I support myself? These resources provide answers to every recovery question you might have and prepare you for a winning battle.

Addict in the Family
Stories of Loss, Hope, and Recovery
by Beverly Conyers

Family stories of addiction that provide lessons and encouragement for families with an addicted loved one.

(Hazelden Publishing, Order No. 1018)

Everything Changes
Help for Families of Newly Recovering Addicts
by Beverly Conyers

This book guides us through the emotional early stages of a loved one's recovery and shows why healthy expectations, support, and boundaries are essential.

(Hazelden Publishing, Order No. 3807)

In the Realm of Hungry Ghosts
Close Encounters with Addiction
by Gabor Maté, MD

In a completely reimagined understanding of addiction, Dr. Gabor Maté leverages his twenty years spent treating addicts on the streets of Vancouver to provide us with a clear and modern interpretation of addiction and why it manifests.

(North Atlantic Books)

It Takes a Family
A Cooperative Approach to Lasting Sobriety
by Debra Jay

Debra Jay teaches us how to create a structured model of family support and collaboration so every member can become a loving part of the recovery team.

(Hazelden Publishing, Order No. 7559)

Not by Chance
How Parents Boost Their Teen's Success In and After Treatment
by Tim Thayne

Therapist and residential treatment professional Tim Thayne highlights the ways in which a young person's healthy recovery is sabotaged and how we, as a family, can encourage, instead of prevent, long-term sobriety.

(Advantage Media Group)

Recovering My Kid
Parenting Young Adults in Treatment and Beyond
by Joseph Lee, MD

Dr. Joseph Lee teaches us how to rebuild our family and our trust in our addicted child, and rally our family around the child's needs and recovery.

(Hazelden Publishing, Order No. 4693)

MEMOIR

You are never alone. Whatever pain you feel, someone else feels too. The voices and victims of addiction are many. These memoirs each tell personal stories of family loss and healing, from which we may all learn and find comfort.

Beautiful Boy
A Father's Journey Through His Son's Addiction
by David Sheff

In this *New York Times* best seller, a helpless father tries desperately to save his beautiful boy before addiction steals him away forever.

(Mariner Books)

The Joey Song
A Mother's Story of Her Son's Addiction
by Sandra Swenson

Author Sandra Swenson learns what it means to let go and find her own peace while her beloved, addicted child refuses all of her attempts to help him get sober.

(Central Recovery Press, LLC)

Mothering Addiction
A Parent's Story of Heartache, Healing, and Keeping the Door Open
by Lynda Harrison Hatcher

Lynda Harrison Hatcher shares the honest pains that result from having a son addicted to heroin and what that journey taught her about her own mental health and self-care.

(Frontier Press)

Saving Jake
When Addiction Hits Home
by D'Anne Burwell

Winner of the 2016 Eric Hoffer Book Award in Memoir, D'Anne Burwell brings us inside a home ravaged by addiction. We see addiction tear the Burwell family apart by the seams while Jake races toward a seemingly inevitable catastrophe.

(FocusUp Books)

Tweak
Growing Up on Methamphetamines
by Nic Sheff

For those looking to learn more about the experiences of an addicted child, this *New York Times* best seller by Nic Sheff, the son of *Beautiful Boy* author David Sheff, is a must-read. Nic shares his experiences in the dark reality of addiction and how, eventually, he is able to escape its death sentence.

(Atheneum Books for Young Readers)

A Very Fine House
A Mother's Story of Love, Faith, and Crystal Meth
by Barbara Cofer Stoefen

Author Barbara Cofer Stoefen learns how to save herself while she battles against her daughter's untiring cycle of meth addiction.

(Zondervan)

Our love for our children will never end. Our lives have centered around their needs since the very start. Using these resources, it's now time to start giving some of our love and comfort back to ourselves.

Codependent No More
How to Stop Controlling Others and Start Caring for Yourself
by Melody Beattie

For those of us who struggle with healthy boundaries, this classic, best-selling book by Melody Beattie teaches us how to stop compromising our own needs and start looking out for our own health and wellness.

(Hazelden Publishing, Order No. 5014)

Conquering Shame and Codependency
8 Steps to Freeing the True You
by Darlene Lancer

For those of us healing from an unhealthy marriage or relationship with an addicted person, Darlene Lancer provides eight actionable steps for overcoming both shame and codependency, helping us to find healthy love and live our best lives.

(Hazelden Publishing, Order No. 7554)

Find Your Light
Practicing Mindfulness to Recover from Anything
by Beverly Conyers

Recovery and wellness expert Beverly Conyers explains why mindfulness is an irreplaceable part of our health and healing toolkit. Whether we are recovering from addiction, codependency, anxiety, disordered eating, or any other behavioral or emotional health issue, this approachable book can help us illuminate the best parts of ourselves. For more mindfulness practice, also look for the follow-up guided journal, *Follow Your Light*.

(Hazelden Publishing, Order No. 3591)

The Grief Club
The Secret to Getting Through All Kinds of Change
by Melody Beattie

Having lost a child of her own, Melody Beattie understands too well the pain of a suffering parent. She channels her experiences and deft writing to gift us a deeply impactful book that helps us move forward from any kind of loss.

(Hazelden Publishing, Order No. 2606)

The Language of Letting Go
Daily Meditations on Codependency
by Melody Beattie

In a convenient daily-reader format, Melody provides us once again with the words and thoughts we need to keep healthy boundaries around our needs and ensure each day is lived to its fullest.

(Hazelden Publishing, Order No. 5076)

A Life of My Own
Meditations on Hope and Acceptance
by Karen Casey

By beloved recovery author Karen Casey, this book of daily meditations helps the loved ones of addicts shift the focus back toward themselves. Inspirational and affirming, each word will give us the strength to heal and grow.

(Hazelden Publishing, Order No. 1070)

Tending Dandelions
Honest Meditations for Mothers with Addicted Children
by Sandra Swenson

In this meditation book created specifically for mothers of addicted children, Sandra Swenson channels her own experiences into a cathartic source of strength and relief for other mothers to rely upon each day.

(Hazelden Publishing, Order No. 3481)

ONLINE RESOURCES

Visit these helpful websites for more valuable information on addiction, mental health disorders, treatment, and recovery, and to join support communities that prove you are not alone.

Addictsmom.com	NAMI.org
Al-anon.org	Nar-anon.org
Drugabuse.gov	Palgroup.org
Drugfree.org	Recoveryanswers.org
Hazeldenbettyford.org	Samhsa.gov
Mompower.org	SMARTrecovery.org

Acknowledgments

There are so many people to thank for their support in making this book.

The sisterhood of TAM has meant everything to me; the support you have all given me has meant so much. I will carry you always.

Beverly, Freddy, Sheree, Rudy, Peter, Nicole, and Alex spent countless hours reading my ideas, helping me sort through both happy and painful family memories, and giving me feedback on what they thought I needed when I was in my deepest stages of grief.

My heart goes out to John Lavitt for the hours of interviews he did with me and my family across several years. Without him, producing books to help families experiencing this disease would never have happened.

The staff at Hazelden Publishing made this book come alive. We share a mission. My sincere gratitude for the late nights and weekends it took to produce this book. Heather Silsbee, Christian Johnson, Terri Kinne, Jean Cook, Don Freeman, Sara Perfetti, Wendy Videen, Chris Deets, Jill Grindahl, and Vanessa Torrado—you are a great team.

Finally, I feel you with me always, Daniel. Thank you for guiding me as I try to help families impacted by this terrible disease.

About the Author

Barbara Theodosiou is a mother, an activist, and the founder of The Addict's Mom, an online community where tens of thousands of mothers of addicted children can "Share Without Shame." Barbara has been widely recognized for her work as a family recovery advocate, including the receipt of a White House Champions of Change award in 2016.

She is the author of *Without Shame: The Addict's Mom and Her Family Share Their Stories of Pain and Healing*. While Barbara is proud of the spotlight she's been able to shine on addiction's impact on families, she is most proud of her roles as a daughter, wife, sister, mother, and friend.

You can join The Addict's Mom community at addictsmom.com or join The Addict's Mom closed group on Facebook.

About Hazelden Publishing

As part of the Hazelden Betty Ford Foundation, Hazelden Publishing offers both cutting-edge educational resources and inspirational books. Our print and digital works help guide individuals in treatment and recovery, and their loved ones. Professionals who work to prevent and treat addiction also turn to Hazelden Publishing for evidence-based curricula, digital content solutions, and videos for use in schools, treatment programs, correctional programs, and electronic health records systems. We also offer training for implementation of our curricula.

Through published and digital works, Hazelden Publishing extends the reach of healing and hope to individuals, families, and communities affected by addiction and related issues.

For more information about Hazelden publications,
please call **800-328-9000**
or visit us online at **hazelden.org/bookstore**.

Other Titles That May Interest You

Tending Dandelions
Honest Meditations for Mothers with Addicted Children
SANDRA SWENSON
2018 Midwest Book Awards Finalist!
In the shadows of our child's struggles with addiction, we find ourselves tending to a life for which we weren't prepared. Yet that place also holds great opportunity for personal growth. These meditations provide encouragement and understanding for those who are realizing that recovery rarely follows a neat or comfortable path.
Order No. 3481, also available as an ebook

Addict in the Family
Stories of Loss, Hope, and Recovery
BEVERLY CONYERS
Witnessing the addiction of a family member is a heart-rending experience. But hope can prevail, as shown in this compelling revised and updated book. In *Addict in the Family,* the gripping stories of fathers, mothers, sons, and daughters of addicts offer important lessons on loving, detachment, intervention, and self-care.
Order No. 1018; also available as an ebook

Everything Changes
Help for Families of Newly Recovering Addicts
BEVERLY CONYERS
Everything Changes assuages fears and uncertainty by teaching loved ones of newly recovering addicts how to navigate the often-tumultuous early months of recovery. Beverly Conyers again shares the hope and knowledge that she gained as the parent of a recovering addict by focusing on the aftermath of addiction. She outlines the physical and psychological changes that recovering addicts go through and offers practical tools to help their family members and friends.
Order No. 3807, also available as an ebook

To order these or other resources from Hazelden Publishing, call **800-328-9000** or visit **hazelden.org/bookstore**.

Millions of mothers struggle silently with an addicted son or daughter. In *Without Shame*, a candid account of the impact of addiction, Barbara pierces both silence and shame, and helps mothers know where to turn.

■ ■ ■ **D'Anne Burwell,** author of *Saving Jake: When Addiction Hits Home*

Without Shame takes us behind closed doors, allowing us to see, feel, and experience the devastating impact that substance use disorders have on the entire family.

■ ■ ■ **Lorelie Rozzano,** author of *Jagged Little Edges, Jagged Little Lies,* and *Jagged No More*

You have made great strides in learning to focus on your own recovery. Now read the story that started a community.

The Addict's Mom
and Her Family
Share Their Stories
of Pain and Healing

without shame

Barbara
Theodosiou

**Founder of The Addict's Mom community and recipient
of a White House Champion of Change award**

In *Without Shame: The Addict's Mom and Her Family Share Their Stories of Pain and Healing,* Barbara Theodosiou, her children, and her husband reveal the pain, loss, and connection that emerge in a family struggling with addiction, trauma, codependency, and recovery. *Without Shame* will show your whole family, that no matter what you have experienced, you are not alone and recovery is possible.